Building Bat Houses

Dale Gelfand

Table of Contents

Introduction

Why, you may be asking yourself, would anyone want to build a bat house?

Mention the word *bat*, and the image that springs to mind for most people is of a bizarre flying beast, a vicious creature — fangs bared, ready to turn into Dracula, spread rabies, or, at the very least, get tangled in your hair.

While it's true that a number of species of bats have some odd characteristics, the unsavory reputation saddled upon these peaceful mammals is the result of age-old myths, fables, and misconceptions. To this day, bats are frequently associated with witchcraft, vampires, and haunted houses, and their fearsome reputation remains unshakable. It's also unjustified. Not only are bats *not* bloodthirsty, they are, in fact, beneficial to human civilization.

Bats rid the world of billions of insect pests every night, and they act as pollinators and seed dispersers for many different plants. But because bats have been so badly and wrongly maligned, whole colonies are still routinely eliminated. In the United States alone, more than 50 percent of our resident bat species are either declining rapidly or listed as endangered. Much of this decrease in bat numbers can be directly attributed to adverse human intervention, be it through direct killing of the animals as a result of ignorance or cruelty, the use of pesticides on their food supply, or the destruction of their habitat. Even unintentional or well-meant disturbances — from spelunkers inadvertently exploring bats' caves or biologists deliberately entering bats' domains to study their habits and habitats — can have severely detrimental effects on hibernating or maternity colonies.

For this reason, there is a growing movement to preserve natural bat habitats or to provide them with artificial roosting sites. Thanks to efforts by conservationists, both governmental and private organizations (foremost among the latter being Bat Conservation International — BCI — a Texas-based nonprofit organization dedicated to bat conservation, research, and public education), more and more people are now willing, even eager, for bats to make nightly forays into their backyards. An excellent way to make neighborhoods attractive to bats is to provide artificial habitats to augment the decreasing natural ones. Besides, it's only right that since bats do so much for us, we do something for them in return.

The Benefits of Bats

Bats are the primary predator of night-flying insects, from mosquitoes that spread disease (not to mention annoyance) to codling moths that attack apple trees and bollworm moths that feast on cotton plants. In fact, in some areas the moths that feed on farm crops make up 90 percent of a bat's diet; in others, the control of malaria has been aided by the resident bat population's diet of mosquitoes.

Big Brown Bats (that's the species' name, not just its description), which live primarily in agricultural areas, feed on June bugs, cucumber beetles, stinkbugs, corn rootworms, grasshoppers, and leafhoppers. Over the course of one summer, a colony of 150 Big Brown Bats will dispatch 38,000 cucumber beetles, 16,000 June bugs, 19,000 stinkbugs, and 50,000 leafhoppers while preventing 18 million corn rootworms from ever seeing the light of day by consuming the beetle stage of this insect pest.

The Little Brown Bat, on the other hand, is a prodigious consumer of mosquitoes. A single Little Brown Bat can eat some 500 mosquitoes in just one hour's time, or nearly 3,000 every night (a bat may consume nearly 50 percent of its body weight in insects nightly); a colony of 100 will likely ingest more than 250,000 mosquitoes a night. Forest-dwelling bats are crucial to maintaining ecosystem health, controlling such pests as tent caterpillar moths

Bat History

The oldest known fossil remains of bats date from the early Eocene period, which means bats have been around for some 50 million years. This makes the bat a remarkably enduring and successful species — by comparison, we humans are mere upstarts, with our earliest ancestors having appeared only about 3.5 million years ago. Yet, oddly, the comparison between our two species is somewhat apt: Not only are both humans and bats warm-blooded mammals that give birth to underdeveloped young that nurse from breasts, but we also both spring from a common ancestor — a shrewlike, pre-Tertiary, forest-dwelling mammal. However, unlike our distant bat kin, we humans decided to stick to terra firma, while they took to the sky.

that in their larval, caterpillar stage would otherwise defoliate huge swaths of forest.

In their aides-to-horticulture guise, bats — like honeybees and hummingbirds — flit from flower to flower, feeding on nectar and pollen or seeking out the insects that crawl inside the blossoms to feed on nectar. In so doing, bats carry pollen and seeds with them, pollinating and dispersing as they go. Their pollination is vital to the existence of many plant species in many different ecosystems, from rain forests to deserts. Bats are the primary pollinators of organ pipe and saguaro cacti, and their seed dispersal assists the propagation of wild bananas, mangoes, dates, figs, peaches, avocados, cashews, and breadfruits. These wild stock of commercial favorites are important genetic sources for developing new disease-resistant strains and reinvigorating old varieties — and they all depend on bats for their propagation and, therefore, survival.

Bats and Human Health

If you like the idea of attracting such helpful creatures to your yard, yet fear the health risks of doing so, you can relax. Probably the biggest health risk that people face from bats is their own fearful reaction to them. More people injure themselves in their frenzied escapes from bats swooping for insects — some have even fallen off docks and boats and almost drowned! — than are ever harmed by bats. Incidentally, the myth of bats flying into people's hair is the result of bats being attracted to the insects that often swarm around our heads.

Blind as a Bat

Despite the expression, bats can indeed see. However, they rely on their hearing — using a highly sophisticated system of ultrasonic sound pulses and echoes called "echolocation," which they emit through their mouths — to navigate and catch prey in total darkness. Like a ship's captain reading sonar, a bat can determine the size, location, density, and movement (if any) of an object in its path.

What about rabies? In fact, bats are the least likely of mammals to transmit the disease; fewer than .05 percent of bats contract rabies, and rabies is very rarely spread within individual colonies. Rabies is much more likely to strike dogs, foxes, skunks, and raccoons, which makes any of these animals a much greater rabies threat than a bat. In the rare instance in which a bat does have rabies, even in its rabid state it will seldom be aggressive — unlike any of the aforementioned species — and will only attack in self-defense, when provoked or threatened. According to BCI, in the last 50 years, fewer than 25 Americans have contracted rabies from bats. Most human exposure to infected bats results from careless handling of grounded bats, so simply following the "never handle a wild animal with your bare hands" rule of thumb will usually keep you out of harm's way. (Of course, not all grounded bats are rabid; young pups often become grounded when they're learning to fly.)

Also, contrary to what you may have heard, bats are not filthy (in fact, they groom themselves much like cats) and won't infest the area with dangerous parasites (most bat parasites are so specialized that they can't survive away from the bats, so they pose little threat to people and other animals). As for histoplasmosis, an airborne disease caused by a microscopic fungus found in bat guano — and that also occurs naturally in soils throughout temperate climates — mounting a bat house away from your dwelling should eliminate any problems resulting from droppings. (Hibernating bats don't produce guano, should you have bats that winter over, either in a bat house or your house.) And far from being aggressive, bats are quite timid and don't attack people or pets.

Attracting Bats

Bat houses are generally constructed for two basic purposes. Smaller boxes with a capacity for up to 100 bats are used to attract males or nonreproductive females. Larger boxes with a capacity for up to 300 or so bats are good for maternity colonies. Inspections of occupied bat houses have determined that about one-third of bat houses are used by nursery colonies, slightly less than two-thirds by bachelor colonies, and the remainder for hibernation in warmer climates. BCI surveyed bat house owners, who reported an overall occupancy rate of approximately 52 percent, with success rates lower for smaller boxes (32 percent) and higher for larger boxes (71 percent).

Winged Friends

Bats are unique in the mammal world. Of all the thousands of mammalian species, they are the only ones that truly fly. (Never mind "flying" squirrels — they merely glide from tree to tree.) However, unlike birds, which flap their wings, bats essentially swim through the air. The name of their mammalian order is *Chiroptera*, which means "flying hand." Interestingly, the bones in a bat's wing are the same as those of the human arm and hand — with the finger bones greatly elongated and connected by a double membrane of skin to form the wing. Like a bird on the wing, a bat will seize its insect prey with its mouth, but when an insect manages to take an evasive action, the bat will catch it by scooping it into its tail or wing membrane — kind of like using a baseball glove — and then lean down and grab the morsel with their teeth. Large prey — dragonflies, katydids, or small vertebrates such as frogs and mice that are taken by carnivorous bats — are disabled with a quick bite, then carried to a perch, the ground, or back to the roost to be eaten.

There are almost 1,000 species of bats worldwide, each with its particular roosting preferences. The social species, which cluster in caves, buildings, and other shelters, are far more likely to roost in bat houses than their forest-dwelling cousins.

Successfully attracting bats requires both patience and experimentation. If more desirable roosts already exist, your thoughtfully provided bat house may remain vacant. A year to year-and-a-half waiting period is common, and some highly successful bat houses take until the third year to acquire tenants. Trying to attract a maternity colony is the more difficult endeavor, because these colonies return year after year to their traditional roosts and usually won't seek out new quarters unless they've been displaced from their customary home. So while it's possible that your intended maternity bat house will be unoccupied for a number of seasons, by erecting a box, you're providing an alternative shelter in the event that a traditional roost is destroyed or sealed off. You should hang the bat box in the fall or winter — before bats come out of hibernation in April and go seeking a roost.

Bat-Proofing Your Home

Attics are the ideal environment for maternity colonies: They're hot and dry and usually predator-free. Two species — the Little Brown Bat and the Big Brown Bat — are particularly fond of attics. Unfortunately, most homeowners don't like sharing their living quarters with these beneficial creatures and often, in their determination to be rid of what they consider a nuisance or a health threat, either vandalize the roosts or exterminate the animals using poisons. But vandalizing a roost doesn't just threaten the resident bat population; it also allows the resident insect population to flourish, because nature's wonderful system of checks and balances has been destroyed. And using poisons not only kills beneficial bats but also scatters dead and dying bats throughout the house and neighborhood.

The safest and most humane way to evict a maternity colony of bats from your attic or other structure is to seal off the entrances once the colony has left for the winter or before it returns the following spring to hopefully take up residence in its new bat box. If you miss this window of opportunity, wait until August, when the pups are old enough to fly, and install one-way doors. *Bat-proofing must never be done during May, June, or July, when the flightless pups are confined in the roost and would be trapped inside.* Doing so would result in dead and decaying pups or pups entering living spaces in search of a way out — as well as frantic mothers attempting to enter your house, even during the day, to rejoin their young.

For fall, winter, or early-spring sealing, the first step in bat-proofing is to locate the points of entry. The most common are joints that have warped or shrunk, leaving gaps; attic vents that have either broken louvers or torn screening; flashing that has pulled away from siding or the roof; broken clapboards; and chimneys. Start by inspecting the ground around the foundation for bat droppings, which accumulate below their entrances. Next, on a sunny day, climb into the attic and see where light is entering from; conversely, put a bright light in the attic and, after dark, stand outside and see where light is shining through. Bats can enter a hole as small as ⅜-inch (10 mm) in diameter, so be diligent.

Once you've identified the entry ports, seal them. Bats can't gnaw new holes or reopen old ones, so once sealed, they'll stay sealed. Caulk cracks near the roofline and gaps where pipes or wires enter the building. Use metal flashing to seal joints in the house, mortar to seal foundation cracks, and weather-stripping to seal cracks around doors and windowsills. Attic vents and louvers should be sealed with ¼-inch (6 mm) hardware cloth to allow for proper ventilation, and bird screens should be installed over chimneys. *Only seal up entrances if you are certain the bats have left your building.*

If you must evict a colony after the pups have begun flying, you can do so by installing one-way "doors" — ¼-inch (6 mm) diameter screening or heavy-duty plastic mesh that allows bats to leave on their nightly insect forays but prevents their reentering at dawn. This simple but effective solution works because when bats return to their roosts, they find their entryways by smell, not sight, which means they'll alight on the screening at the point of the opening, not below it. Screening or mesh is inexpensive and available at most garden shops or hardware stores.

Dr. Stephen Frantz, a research scientist for the New York State Department of Health, has studied bats and bat houses extensively. He has developed a plan for one-way doors that is safe and effective (see box below).

One-Way Door Installation

1. Using ¼-inch (6 mm) wire screening or heavy-duty plastic mesh, cut enough material so that it bows out 3 to 5 inches (8 to 13 cm) and completely covers the opening. The screening should extend about 3 feet (90 cm) beneath the hole.
2. Tape the screening in place with duct tape or exterior staples, leaving the bottom open.
3. Leave the door in place for at least four days, or until you're sure that all the bats have left; then remove the one-way door and seal the opening.

Never use a one-way door during May, June, or July to ensure that no pups will be trapped inside and die.

Bat Species Distribution

Nine species of bats that are known to use bat houses are:

Species	Territory	Roosts
Little Brown Bat *(Myotis lucifugus)*	Wooded areas throughout most of Canada and northern half of U.S., except desert and arid areas	Rears young in tree hollows, buildings, rock crevices, and bat houses; most common species to occupy bat houses
Big Brown Bat *(Eptesicus fuscus)*	Most of U.S. and Canada, except extreme southern Florida	Rears young in tree hollows and buildings; Hibernates in caves, abandoned mines, and buildings; frequent bat house user; may overwinter in bat houses from Texas to New York
Southeastern Bat *(Myotis austroriparius)*	Gulf States, primarily	Rears young in caves, tree hollows, and buildings; hibernates in caves in northern range and tree hollows or buildings farther south; uses bat houses in Gulf States
Yuma Bat *(Myotis yumanensis)*	Western Canada, Washington, Idaho, Oregon, California, Arizona, extreme western Nevada, eastern Utah, and southern Colorado to western New Mexico	Rears young in caves, in buildings, and under bridges; occupies bat houses from Arizona to southwestern Canada

Northern Long-Eared Bat, Eastern Long-Eared Bat *(Myotis septentrionalis)*	Upper Midwest and east into Canada; south into northern Arkansas, Tennessee, western Alabama, and eastern Georgia	Rears young beneath tree bark, in buildings, and in bat houses; summers beneath tree bark, in buildings, and in caves; hibernates in rock crevices, caves, and mines
Evening Bat *(Nycticeius humeralis)*	East of Appalachian Mountains: from southern Pennsylvania to Florida; west of Appalachian Mountains: north to southern Michigan and Wisconsin, west to southeastern Nebraska, and south to southeastern Texas	Rears young in buildings, tree cavities, and bat houses; shares nursery colonies with Mexican Free-Tailed Bats
Pallid Bat *(Antrozous pallidus)*	Western and southwestern U.S., mostly in arid areas	Summers in rock crevices, buildings, bat houses, and under bridges; hibernates in deep rock crevices
Cave Bat *(Myotis velifer)*	Southern Arizona and New Mexico into western Texas and Oklahoma, and extreme south-central Kansas	Rears young in caves and building crevices; shares bat houses with Mexican Free-Tailed Bats in Texas
Brazilian Free-Tailed Bat, Mexican Free-Tailed Bat *(Tadarida brasiliensis)*	Southern and southwestern U.S., and north to Nebraska, Colorado, Utah, Nevada, and Oregon	Rears young in caves, buildings, bat houses, and under bridges; migrates to Mexican and Central American caves for winter, except in Florida

Bat House Construction

Like birds, bats are fussy about their living quarters. It's hard to predict whether the bats in your area will want to move into a bat house that you provide for them. For one thing, shelter is but a third of the essential bat-needs equation, the other two elements being water and an ample food supply.

Location, Location, Location

A nearby permanent water source (a lake, stream, marsh, or river within ¼ mile, or about 400 m) is ideal for bat habitation. Almost guaranteeing colonization would be adding a combination of nearby fruit orchards, other agricultural endeavors, and natural vegetation. But even if your house isn't within sight of a lake, 100 yards away from an apple orchard, and across the street from a potato farm, you can attract bats if roosts are needed and your bat house meets bat requirements.

Foremost is orienting the box so that it receives enough sunlight in attracting bats to your bat house each day to provide the necessary solar radiation. A recent Pennsylvania State University study found that, at their latitude, all the bat boxes that faced southeast or southwest — so that they received at least seven hours of direct sunlight during the spring and summer — were successful in housing maternity colonies. More northerly areas will likely need to receive more than the seven hours recommended by Pennsylvania State University; more southerly ones can make do with less.

Bat nurseries require a stable temperature of 85 to 100°F (29 to 38°C) for the pregnant females and growing pups, and some species tolerate temperatures as high as 120°F (49°C). In most areas of the North American continent other than the Deep South and the desert Southwest, you don't have to worry about your bat house getting too hot; more likely you'll have to be concerned that it isn't warm enough. (Depending on your location, the air temperature even on hot summer days may well be affected by wind, clouds, and elevation. If you live in a area whose average July temperature is 95°F, or 35°C, but your specific site is on a hillside that gets buffeted by prevailing winds, you should paint your bat house a darker color to compensate for the heat loss.) However, a bat house also needs cooler chambers for the bats to move into in case temperatures do get too high. Attaching black roofing paper to the upper portions of the box, using a tin roof, and cutting a sufficient number of ventilation slits will all greatly reduce overheating.

Also crucial in determining the box site is factoring in whether it's intended to house a displaced maternity colony. If this is the case, the box should be placed as close as possible to the old roost — within 10 to 20 feet (3 to 6 m) — either on the side of a building, a chimney, or a pole. Once the bats have accepted the bat house as their new roost, it can be moved gradually away from the old site *but only during the fall or winter when the bats aren't present.* Don't move the box more than 20 yards (18 m) per year.

When a box is meant to attract a new colony into the area, the ideal site is 12 to 20 feet up on a pole or building, preferably at least 20 feet (4 to 6 m) away from trees, facing south, with an approach unobstructed by vegetation or utility wires, and sheltered from prevailing winds. (Consider mounting four houses in a group, each facing in a different direction to provide a range of temperatures for bats to select from.)

According to a BCI study, houses located on poles, which generally receive more sun and therefore better solar heating, were 81 percent occupied; houses on buildings, 73 percent occupied; houses on trees, 34 percent. Additionally, mounting a bat house high on a pole keeps it safer from predators, and positioning the pole at least 20 feet (6 m) from trees keeps it safer from owls, who, without nearby perches to alight on, can't easily pick off bats as they leave and reenter their roosts. If attaching a box to a tree is your only option, make certain that the leafy canopy won't interfere with the requisite sunlight.

If the box is hung on a building, don't place it in a heavily trafficked area or where droppings will pose a problem, and make sure there's at least 3 feet (90 cm) of open space beneath it so that bats can easily exit; unlike birds, which can take flight from a standstill, most bats need to drop from a perch and catch air beneath their wings before they can fly. To prevent people from walking underneath the bat house, you might consider putting decorative fencing around it or planting some ornamental ground cover such as pachysandra or periwinkle (myrtle) that will discourage foot traffic.

Timing Is Everything

Whether you're installing a bat box to attract a new colony or as a new home for a colony in an existing but undesirable roost — say, your attic — the best times for box placement are between January and April or in the fall when they leave for their winter hibernation. Bats come out of hibernation in March and usually arrive at their summer roosts in April. But since in many areas trees are leafless at this time, a location that receives plenty of sunshine in February might be in full shade come June, so house placement might require some preplanning. It might be better to hang a box after a colony disbands at the end of the summer or early fall, when trees are still in full leaf.

When you're looking to move a colony out of a traditional roost, allow the bats to familiarize themselves with their new home, if possible, before expelling them from their old one. Which is to say, let them investigate the new quarters over the course of the summer while they stay in your attic, and in the fall, when they leave for their winter hibernation, you can bat-proof your house so that when they return the following spring, they may well take up residence in the bat box.

If allowing them to remain for another summer isn't an option, install the bat house and bat-proof your own house before the bats arrive in April. Since colonies in part use smell to identify their roosts, consider scenting the new box with their droppings before putting the box in place. To do so, gather a cup of guano from your attic — bat droppings are dry, black, about the size of grains of rice, and accumulated in piles, unlike mouse droppings, which are scattered — and mix with water to a watery-paste consistency; then pour the mixture into the box, allowing it to soak in before hanging the box. *Note:* Wear rubber gloves and a paper filter mask.

As a less odious alternative, some people have had success "aging" their bat boxes by filling them with slightly damp soil for a few days, then dumping out the soil. If scenting the box isn't possible, and new materials are used for construction, allow the box to weather outside for a while before installation to eliminate that new-box smell. You'll be surprised what a difference scenting a box can make in your success rate.

Predator Guards

To better ward off climbing raccoons and snakes, you can purchase commercial predator guards or make your own by wrapping the bottom of the pole — or tree, for that matter — with a length of sheet metal 1½ to 2 feet (40 to 60 cm) wide and some 3 feet (90 cm) off the ground.

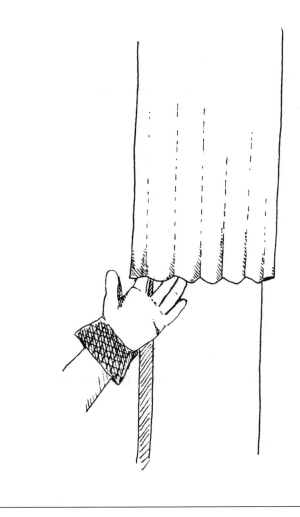

Proper Design

Building a bat house begins with a suitable design.

Size: Maternity colonies require boxes that are at least 24 inches (60 cm) high and 12 inches (30 cm) wide. Smaller houses will be accepted by male bats or nonreproductive females.

Landing board: Whether large or small, all bat houses need landing boards that extend 3 to 6 inches (8 to 15 cm) below the entrance, preferably covered with ⅛- or ¼-inch (3 or 6 mm) plastic mesh or hardware cloth.

Opening: Open bottoms are recommended — contrary to European houses, which generally have a bottom — because they won't need to be regularly cleaned of accumulated droppings and parasites, and birds and rodents won't be tempted to take up residence. (Wasps are the only uninvited guests you'll have to worry about; clean out their nests prior to bat occupancy.)

Crevices: Of primary importance is the interior construction, which utilizes carefully spaced baffles, or partitions, to create multiple roosting chambers, or crevices. These crevices allow for larger populations (sardines in a can have nothing on bats in a box) and also regulate and maintain the proper temperature. The designs (see pages 20–26) provided by Pennsylvania State University contain six crevices, which is the maximum recommended by BCI.

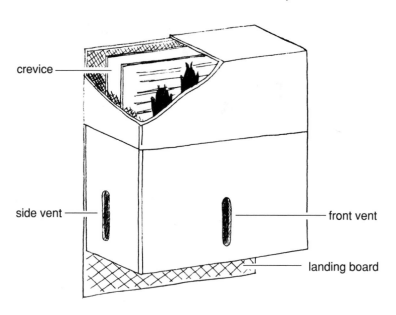

crevice

side vent — front vent

landing board

Vents: Vents are critical in bat houses installed in areas where the average high temperature in July is 85°F (29°C) or greater because they modify interior heating, contributing to bat house success in moderate or hot climates. Keeping these vents to ½-inch-wide (13 mm) spaces will thwart both unwanted light and avian intruders. A front vent, 3 inches (8 cm) long, should be cut vertically about 3 inches (8 cm) up from the bottom, and two other 3 inch (8 cm) long vents should be cut at either end of the rear chamber of multiple-chambered houses. When maternity houses are paired back to back, an additional ¾-inch-wide (19 mm) horizontal vent should be cut in the rear, allowing bats to go back and forth between the two houses without having to exit and reenter.

Proper Materials

Bats seem to show a slight preference for houses that have been constructed of old wood, which, of course, is also environmentally sound. Pennsylvania State University recommends using ¾-inch exterior plywood for the front and back pieces and 1-inch board lumber of western red cedar, pine, or cypress for the sides and spacers. The interior baffles — made from ¼-inch plywood — are thinner than the front and back pieces, and they should be roughened to give the bats a good foothold. As an alternative to filing these surfaces, you can attach ⅛- or ¼-inch (3 or 6 mm) heavy-duty plastic mesh or hardware to the baffles and landing board with ⁵⁄₁₆-inch (8 mm) durable galvanized exterior-grade staples. Pennsylvania State University suggests using ½ to ¾-inch exterior plywood for the roof.

To join the pieces, use 1⅝-inch (41 mm) multipurpose (drywall) screws or galvanized finishing nails and seal them with latex siliconized caulk. Black roofing paper should be applied to the top portion of the box exterior to create a variance in temperature within the crevices. Bat houses mounted in areas where average daily temperatures in July are 80 to 85°F (27 to 29°C) or less should be painted with black exterior latex paint. They should be painted brown, gray, or green where temperatures are 85 to 95°F (29 to 35°C); light brown where they are 95 to 100°F (35 to 37°C); and white where they exceed 100°F (39°C).

Basic Assembly Instructions

These instructions apply to each of the three bat house designs featured in this bulletin. Assembly techniques are the same for each of the designs, only the dimensions of the pieces differ.

1. Cut pieces according to plans. Using a jigsaw, cut 3" x ½" (8cm x 13mm} vents in the front and side pieces (see designs).
2. Use a knife, saw, or router to roughen all interior surfaces with horizontal scratches or grooves ¼ to ½ inch (6 to 13 mm) apart. It's especially important that the landing board, which is the bottom portion of the back piece, is textured. Attaching a piece of plastic netting to the back and baffles using galvanized staples also gives bats a strong foothold. Make sure that the netting lies flat and does not pucker.
3. Attach the sides to the front using wood screws, caulking first. (*Do not use wood glue* on any part of the bat box, as it can be toxic to bats.)
4. Attach the roof to the sides and front using wood screws. Caulk the seams to seal the roosting chamber.
5. Position the box so that the front rests on a tabletop and the sides and roof extend upward.
6. Attach two interior spacer strips to the inside of the front piece using finishing nails or wood screws. Make sure the strips fit tightly against the roof and side pieces.
7. Place one of the shorter baffles on top of the spacer strips, butting it against the roof piece. Attach the baffle to the spacers using finishing nails.
8. Attach two interior spacer strips to the first baffle using finishing nails or wood screws. Make sure the strips fit tightly against the sides of the box.

Tools

- Table saw
- Jig saw
- Variable speed reversing drill
- Phillips-head drill bit
- Tape measure

- Caulking gun
- Scissors
- Heavy-duty stapler
- Paintbrush
- Sander (optional)
- Router (optional)

9. Place one of the longer baffles on top of the spacer strips, butting it against the roof piece. Attach the baffle to the spacers using finishing nails.
10. Repeat steps 7, 8, and 9 (alternating baffle lengths) until all baffles and spacer strips have been installed.
11. Attach the back of the box to the roof and sides using wood screws, caulking the seams. The back piece should extend below the body of the box to serve as the landing board.
12. Paint or stain the exterior using a latex-based paint or stain. *(Do not stain the interior.)* Apply a second coat of paint or stain.
13. Attach roofing paper to the roof. Caulk the seam at the back where the roof attaches to the back panel.
14. Tack roofing paper onto the front and sides, extending it approximately 6 inches (15 cm) down from the top. This will help create differences in temperature from the top of the box to the bottom.

Router Option

If you have a router: After attaching the sides, cut ¼-inch (6 mm) vertical grooves in the side pieces with a router at 1-inch (25 mm) intervals. Skip the instructions for installing spacer strips and baffles. Instead, simply fit the baffles into the side-piece grooves. Then attach the front, back, and roof as described.

Bat House Plans

Plans for the bat boxes that follow were developed by Pennsylvania State University. BCI features similar bat house designs in its publication, *The Bat House Builder's Handbook.*

Small Bat House

Capacity: 50 Bats

This bat box should be useful when trying to attract bats to an area. It may be accepted by male bats or nonreproductive females, although it's not large enough for most bat colonies.

Pieces for Bat House

Part	Quantity	Dimension	Material
front	1	12" x 12" (30cm x 30cm)	¾" exterior plywood
sides	2	12" x 7¾ " (30cm x 19cm)	1" board lumber
roof	1	12" x 8½" (30cm x 22cm)	½"–¾" exterior plywood
spacer strips	10	1" x 10" (25mm x 25cm)	1" board lumber
baffles (with spacers)	3	10" x 10" (25cm x 25cm)	¼" plywood
	2	11" x 10 ½" (28cm x 27cm)	¼" plywood
baffles (if routered)	3	10" x 11" (25cm x 28cm)	¼" plywood
	2	11" x 11" (28cm x 28cm)	¼" plywood
back/landing board	1	18" x 12" (46cm x 30cm)	¾" exterior plywood

Front View

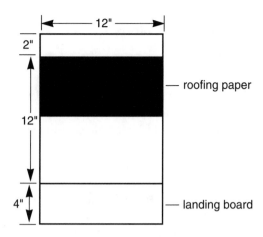

12"

2"

roofing paper

12"

4"

landing board

Side View

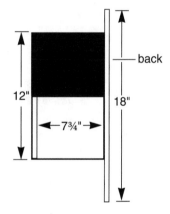

12"

7¾"

back

18"

Cutaway View

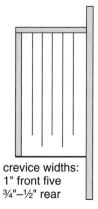

crevice widths:
1" front five
¾"–½" rear

Small Maternity Colony Bat House

Capacity: 150 Bats

This bat box is suitable for small to medium-sized summer maternity colonies (up to 150 bats). If the box is intended to house an evicted colony, it should be installed in the spring *before* the colony is evicted from its current roost.

Pieces for Bat House

Part	Quantity	Dimension	Material
front	1	12" x 24" (30cm x 61cm)	¾" exterior plywood
sides	2	12" x 7¾" (30cm x 19cm)	1" board lumber
roof	1	24" x 8½" (61cm x 22cm)	½"–¾" exterior plywood
spacer strips	10	1" x 10" (25mm x 25cm)	1" board lumber
baffles (with spacers)	3	10" x 22½" (25cm x 57cm)	¼" plywood
	2	11" x 22 ½" (28cm x 57cm)	¼" plywood
baffles (if routered)	3	10" x 23" (25cm x 58cm)	¼" plywood
	2	11" x 23" (28cm x 58cm)	¼" plywood
back/landing board	1	18" x 24" (46cm x 61cm)	¾" exterior plywood

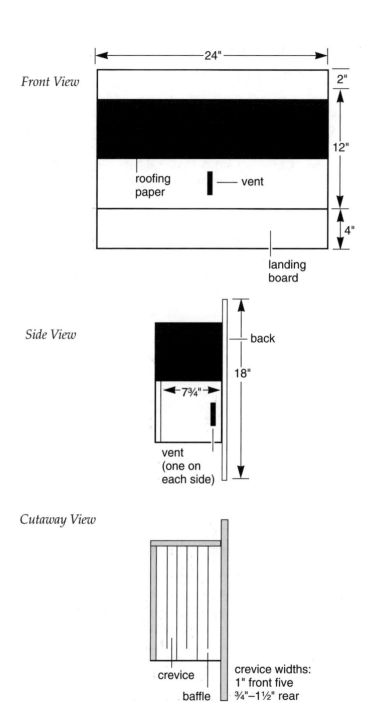

Front View

24"

2"

12"

roofing paper

vent

4"

landing board

Side View

back

18"

7¾"

vent (one on each side)

Cutaway View

crevice

baffle

crevice widths: 1" front five ¾"–1½" rear

Large Maternity Colony Bat Box

Capacity: 150–300 Bats

This bat box is suitable for large summer maternity colonies of up to 300 bats. If the box is intended to house an evicted colony, it should be installed in the spring *before* the colony is evicted from its current roost. If a colony larger than 300 bats is to be evicted, two boxes can be installed side by side, or a larger bat box can be used.

Pieces for Bat House

Part	Quantity	Dimension	Material
front	1	24" x 24" *(61cm x 61cm)*	¾" exterior plywood
sides	2	24" x 7¾" *(61cm x 19cm)*	1" board lumber
roof	1	24" x 8½" *(61cm x 22cm)*	½"–¾" exterior plywood
spacer strips	10	1" x 22" *(25mm x 56cm)*	1" board lumber
baffles (with spacers)	3	22" x 22½" *(56cm x 57cm)*	¼" plywood
	2	23" x 22 ½" *(58cm x 57cm)*	¼" plywood
baffles (if routered)	3	22" x 23" *(56cm x 58cm)*	¼" plywood
	2	23" x 23" *(58cm x 58cm)*	¼" plywood
back/landing board	1	30" x 24" *(76cm x 61cm)*	¾" exterior plywood

Front View

24"

2"

roofing paper

18"

vent

4"

landing
board

Side View

7¾"

24"

vent
(one on
each side)

Cutaway View

crevice widths:
1" front five
¾"–1½" rear

Optional Bat House Modifications

- Wider bat houses can be built for larger colonies by adjusting the dimensions for the back and front pieces, roof, partitions, roof supports, and netting. Additional spacers may be required in the center of the roosting chamber for bat houses more than 24 inches (61 cm) wide. More plywood will be necessary.

- Taller bat houses can be created by adjusting the dimensions of the front and back pieces, partitions, sides, spacers, and netting. Bat houses 3 feet (91 cm) or taller should have a horizontal vent slot 12 inches (30 cm) from the bottom of the roosting chamber.

- Longer landing platforms (up to 12 inches, or 30 cm) can be substituted. They still should be covered with plastic netting.

- Two bat houses can be mounted back to back on poles. Before assembly, a horizontal ¾-inch (19 mm) slot should be cut in the back of each house about 12 inches (30 cm) up from the bottom edge of the back piece to improve ventilation and permit movement between houses. Two pieces of wood 4" x 10¾" x ¾" (10 cm x 25 cm x 1.9 cm), screwed horizontally to each side, will join the two boxes. A single 4" x 23" (10 cm x 58 cm) vertical piece attached to each side over the horizontal pieces blocks light but allows bats and air to enter. Leave a ¾-inch (19 mm) space between the two boxes, and roughen the wood surfaces or cover the back of each with plastic netting. Do not cover the vents. A tin roof covering both houses protects them and helps prevent overheating. Eaves should be about 3 inches (6 cm) in southern areas and about 1½ inch (40 mm) in the north.

- Bat house roofs can be slanted by cutting the top of the side pieces at an angle and sanding off the baffles for a tight fit. A slanted roof will promote water runoff.

- Ventilation may not be necessary in colder climates. Far northern bat houses may also benefit from a partial bottom to help retain heat. Leave a ¾-inch (19 mm) entry gap at the back, and be sure the bottom doesn't interfere with access to the front crevices. A hinged bottom and regular maintenance is required to prevent guano buildup.

Bat-Proofing Materials and Suppliers

Sealing Materials

Expanding Foam Insulation/Caulking Compound
Found in most building supply stores, expanding foam insulation is available as an aerosol and can be sprayed into cracks and crevices. The foam expands to fill the opening and then hardens, after which it can be trimmed or painted.

"Flashband"
"Flashband" is a self-adhesive, aluminum-faced sealant that permanently adheres to almost any surface. It can be useful for sealing roof junctions, loose flashing, eaves, and gaps between chimneys and walls. It's easily applied, requires no special tools, and resists water, rust, mold, and mildew. Contact:

The 3E Group
850 Glen Avenue
P.O. Box 392
Moorestown, NJ 08057-0392
(609) 866-7600

Copper Mesh
Copper cleaning mesh is a rolled, flattened strip of knitted copper mesh, similar to flattened steel wool, that can be cut to any length. It won't rust and is excellent for stuffing into cracks and crevices in buildings. Contact:

Otto H. York Co., Inc.
Attn: Industrial Mesh Division
42 lntervale Road
Parsippany, NJ 07006
(201) 299-9200

"Stuff-It"

"Stuff-it" is a copper gauze product useful for plugging holes that are too big to caulk and too small to warrant carpentry repair (such as openings around eaves). It won't rust, stain, or break down. Contact:

Allen Special Products, Inc.
P.O. Box 605
Montgomeryville, PA 18936
(800) 848-6805

Chimney Caps

Designed to prevent damage to chimneys and fireplaces from rain and snow, chimney caps also can be effective at keeping bats out of your home. Contact:

Chim-a-lator Co.
8824 Wentworth Avenue South
Bloomington, MN 55420
(612) 884-7274

Vestal Manufacturing
P.O. Box 420
Sweetwater, TN 37874
(615) 337-6125

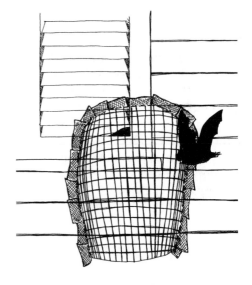

This one-way door is just one of the many products available to help you bat proof your home.

One-Way Door Materials

Metal Hardware Cloth/Screening/Heavy-Duty Bird Netting

Available from most garden supply or hardware stores. Any material used for one-way doors should have a mesh opening no larger than ¼ inch (6 cm). (Mesh diameter is measured on the diagonal, from corner to corner.) Bats can crawl through anything larger and reenter the building. For heavy-duty plastic netting (also useful in bat house construction) and fastener clips, contact:

InterNet, Inc.
2730 Nevada Avenue North
Minneapolis, MN 55247
(800) 328-8456

"Bat Net"

The "Bat Net" kit contains a 14' x 20' (4m x 6m) piece of structural-grade bird netting with Velcro fasteners for attachment to buildings. This company also sells rolls of netting for making one-way doors of any size. Contact:

Wildlife Control Technology, Inc.
2513 Girdwood Road
Timonium, MD 21093
(410) 252-4635

"Bat Check Valve"

The "Bat Check Valve" kit includes a 7' x 14' (2m x 4m) length of structural-grade bird netting, including mounting clips and installation instructions. The company also sells rolls of netting for making one-way doors of any size. Contact:

Wildlife Management Supplies
40 Starkweather
Plymouth, MI 48170
(800) 451-6544

Diatomaceous Earth

Diatomaceous earth, which scratches the cuticle of insects as they crawl through it, is useful in eliminating bat parasites from an attic after the bats have been evicted.

"Shell Shock"

"Shell Shock" is one of several diatomaceous earth products on the market. It comes from fossilized deposits of microscopic shells produced by one-celled plants called diatoms. Contact:

D & R, Inc.
136 Elm Street
South Williamsport, PA 17701
(717) 322-4885

Perma-Guard

"Perma-Guard" kills insects physically, by puncturing their exoskeleton, disrupting their soft, waxy structure, causing death in a short time by dehydration. Contact:

Fossil Shell Company
P.O. Box 50225
Amarillo, TX 79159

Bat Conservation Resources

Bat Conservation International
P.O. Box 162603
Austin, TX 78716

The Lubee Foundation, Inc.
1309 N.W. 192nd Avenue
Gainesville, FL 32609

Pennsylvania State University
College of Agricultural Sciences
Cooperative Extension
University Park, PA 16802

Organization for Bat Conservation
2300 Epley Road
Williamston, MI 48895

Bat Conservation Society of Canada
P.O. Box 56042, Airways Postal Outlet
Calgary, Alberta
T2E 8K5

Conservationists agree that
bat houses are key to
preserving bat populations.

Acknowledgments

The author wishes to thank Bat Conservation International (BCI) for their continued research on bats and bat house construction. Founded in 1982 by Dr. Merlin D. Tuttle, BCI is recognized as the international leader in conservation initiatives that protect bats and their habitats. BCI offers memberships in their conservation efforts and welcomes volunteers for their North American Bat House Research Project.

The author also wishes to thank the Cooperative Extension of Pennsylvania State University for providing the bat house designs featured in this bulletin. The Cooperative Extension can provide further information on larger bat box designs and additional resources.